ROSES
HOW TO KNOW AND GROW THEM

With an introduction by Claudia Binelli

GOLDEN PRESS  **NEW YORK**
Western Publishing Company, Inc.

CONTENTS

Acknowledgments for the use of photographs are due to the following sources:
Archivio B, Milan: 46, 47, 106
Armstrong Nurseries, California (photos, C. Bryant): 34, 98
Conard-Pyle Co, Pennsylvania: 95
E. Dulevant, Turin: 5, 8
Fratelli Ingegnoli, Milan: 7, 13, 14, 31, 35, 56, 67, 85, 87, 88, 100, 121, 124, 125
Germain's Inc, California: 3, 33
Gregory's Roses, Nottingham: 10–12, 15–28, 32, 37–43, 45, 52, 53, 54, 57, 59, 61–66, 68, 73–82, 84, 89–94, 115, 116, 118–120
Kayebon Press Ltd, Cheshire: 9, 49, 50, 72, 96, 97, 99, 102–105, 108–113
G. Mazza, Milan: 3, 60, 117
S. McGredy Roses, Portadown (photos Kayebon Press): 48, 51, 69–71, 101, 107, 114, 122, 123
M. Pasotti, Garda: 2
SEF, Turin: 1, 36, 44
G. Tomsich, Rome: 4, 6, 29, 30, 55, 58, 83
Transworld: 86
Illustrations by Hugh Robson on pages 12–13 are reproduced from *Roses* by Peter Coats (Weidenfeld & Nicolson).

Translated from the Italian of Claudia Binelli

Published in 1972 by Golden Press, New York, a division of Western Publishing Company, Inc.

© Orbis Publishing Limited, London 1971
© Istituto Geografico de Agostini, Novara 1967

Printed in Italy by IGDA, Novara

Library of Congress Catalog Card Number: 72-166530

Another book on roses? Any rose-lover who sees a new publication in the shops may be inclined to wonder how it can possibly be justified. At first glance, you might think there was nothing new to be said, no new problem to be studied, so fully have roses been dealt with by distinguished botanists and artists. But if you consider that about fifteen thousand species are being cultivated today, and two hundred new varieties are shown at international competitions every year, if you think of their commercial importance, of the thousands of acres on which they are grown all over the world, of their beauty both out of doors and in the house, it becomes clear that there is plenty more to be said about them.

This book deals first of all with the remarkable history of the rose from ancient times until our own day, and with what it has symbolised in the history of man. Country-lovers will find descriptions of wild species that anyone may find to admire in the hedgerows, wild species that are the ancestors of many varieties of cultivated roses.

The origin of the cultivated rose is another fascinating subject. Imaginative growers have, down the years, managed to obtain a very wide range of colour, and today, with all the scientific means at their disposal, and by the skilful crossing of roses, they are still patiently trying to produce a black or a blue rose.

Then, all down the centuries, both the flower and the fruit of the roses have had various uses, and today they are still used in the making of scents and cosmetics and medicinal products. They are commercially important as well, of course, as cut flowers, potted plants, and for display in the garden or in the house. Anyone wanting to grow roses in his garden or on a balcony in town will find advice on how to do so and on the diseases from which they may suffer.

The importance of the rose in art is also briefly discussed; painters and, even more so, engravers, have found it a constant source of inspiration.

There are many illustrations, with very full captions, which means that every part of the text is easy to follow and the best known species and varieties can be recognised.

The rose needs no introduction: its fresh, abundant petals, its superb colour, its delicate scent and exquisite form all make it a truly regal flower. Every garden, however modest, needs to have roses in it. In fact, it is impossible to imagine the world without the rose, for it has been adorning the earth since time immemorial, cheering man from his earliest years and often serving as a symbol of some aspect of his history.

This book is dedicated to all who love roses, and who have found in them the wonderful harmony and beauty in which nature is steeped.

'The man with a rose in his hat', says a Mexican proverb, 'has the whole world' – because he has known the beauty of creation, and, in gazing at it, is happy.

Claudia Binelli

Rosa gallica

Published by Dr Woodville May 1 1792.

The rose in religion and symbolism

From the earth's earliest days until the time of Christ, from the Middle Ages until our own day, the rose has been part of man's life on earth, and its origins are lost in legend and in mythology. All we know for certain is that it originated in central Asia, spreading eastwards to North America, and westwards to Asia Minor and Europe, but never crossing the equator.

In India they say the most beautiful woman in the world, the goddess Lakshmi, was born from a large rose, and in the East the rose was sacred to the goddess of fertility, whose priestesses wore wreaths of white roses on their heads. Confucius says there were rose gardens in ancient China and Japan, and a Chinese manuscript on roses is dated 500 BC.

The Incas in Peru, before the Spanish Conquest, grew them and called the rose-tree 'the bush of the sun'. When Christopher Columbus reached the West Indies he found roses there. But the real home of the rose in the ancient world was Persia: whole gardens were given over to it, superb rose-trees surrounded the city, the emperors themselves were skilled gardeners, and, in the luxurious Persian tradition, rich crowns were made of rose-petals stitched with raffia.

From Persia the rose was brought to Babylonia, where it was grown in the famous Hanging Gardens and became a symbol of the power of the state. There, Jewish prisoners came to know and love it. But it came very much later into Egypt and Asia Minor, and flowers that are called roses in many ancient translations should in fact be called lilies.

The rose reached Greece in the fifth century BC, and Epicurus admired it. Homer never knew it, but Sappho called it, for the first time, 'the queen of flowers'. In Greek mythology it was said that Cybele created the rose because she was jealous of Aphrodite – and wished to create something more beautiful than the goddess of beauty herself. But when Aphrodite rushed to the wounded Adonis, tearing through a rose hedge and staining the flowers with her blood, the red rose was born. So the rose became the symbol of Aphrodite and of Aurora and Cupid, who accompanied her, representing love and its fleeting nature, and youth. It was also sacred to Harpocrates, the god of silence.

The Greeks were the first to use the expression that was later latinised to 'sub rosa', under the rose, to mean something secret and mysterious. This expression seems to have been used for the first time during preparations for the decisive battle of the Greeks against the Persians, which were made very secretly in a bower of roses, and although we cannot know for certain whether this story is true, we do know that the rose became a symbol of secrecy and that the term 'sub rosa' came down from ancient times into the Middle Ages, and spread all over Europe. Indeed, if a conversation were to take place in secret, a rose was hung on the ceiling, although, later on, this rose came to be made of plaster.

The Greeks considered it a flower for weddings, as well, and the women made crowns of roses, interwoven with branches of myrtle. But if it was worn on the brow or the breast, it was a sign of mourning.

From Greece the rose passed on to Rome, where it enjoyed a further period of splendour. In the early years of the Roman republic, roses were made into crowns which were worn by heroes and defenders of the state, and when the republic was in danger the wearing of roses was strictly forbidden. But later this changed, and under the Emperor Augustus roses were used in every type of decoration.

At feasts and banquets everyone, old and young, slaves, musicians and dancers, wore crowns of roses stitched with raffia; roses were twined around goblets, rose-petals dropped into the wine when toasts were drunk, and the cushions the guests sat on were filled with rose petals. Roses were used in the preparation of jellies, honey and wine, and rose petals were eaten crystallised.

The rose-gardens of Paestum became famous, attracting large crowds when they were in flower, and were praiséd by Virgil and Ovid. The Romans also looked on the rose as a

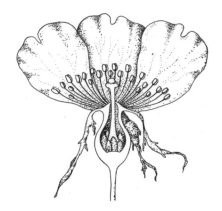

Line drawing of a wild rose flower: a simple flower, like that of the dog rose.

Section of a wild rose flower.

symbol of love and used it to decorate their graves. In April and May, during the feast of Flora, goddess of flowers, they held celebrations in honour of the rose, and often mentioned in their wills the kinds of roses they wanted on their graves, and left bequests of money for their planting and upkeep.

Gradually, however, the Romans' pleasure in roses became luxuriant folly. The peasants cut down their orchards and olive groves to make space for them, elaborate hothouses were built to allow them to bloom in winter, and they were brought across from Egypt by sea. Unfortunately, we know nothing about the methods by which they were transported, methods which somehow allowed them to arrive in Rome still fresh. It would seem, indeed, that the Romans' extravagance over roses was something they learned from Egypt, where Cleopatra spent vast sums in order to surround herself with roses. Suetonius says that Nero spent the equivalent of about £50,000 on roses for a single banquet; so the Romans were clearly not far behind her in lavish expense.

With the coming of Christianity this extravagance came to an end; indeed, for a short time the rose was forbidden and forgotten. But soon it returned to favour and became the loveliest decoration of the churches on religious feasts. Once again it was used as a symbol of secrecy, and in 1500 Pope Hadrian had a rose carved on all confessionals, where for some time it had been the custom to hang a real rose that had been blessed.

It seems that the prayer beads St. Dominic called 'rosaries' in 1208, which are still an object of devotion today, were first made from rose hips.

Legends grew up around the rose and many people used it symbolically. The Turks, for instance, say that the white rose originated from Mohammed's sweat and the red rose from his blood; so it is the sacred flower of the Mohammedans and until about 1750 it was the custom to wrap the babies of the Seraglio in rose-petals.

When the Roman empire in the west was overwhelmed by the barbarians, the Arabs carried on the traditions of the Persian and Babylonian gardeners and used roses extravagantly, like the ancient Romans. From about the year 1000, they managed to extract essences from roses, and to make rose-water through distillation; these scents were used to purify the mosques and other religious rooms. When North Africa and Spain were conquered the Arabs passed their love of roses on to their subject peoples.

Flowers were not considered important in the Middle Ages: people were too busy fighting and too many necessities were lacking for them to worry about the luxuries of life. But if the rose fell from favour as an ornament, it became important for its medicinal properties. Its fruit, which was rich in vitamin C, was an excellent remedy against scurvy, the most widespread of medieval diseases, and so it was grown in monasteries and spread all over Europe by the Benedictines.

It was only in France and England that the love of roses never died, in spite of wars and revolutions, and so it was in those two countries that the modern rose came into being. In France, at Fontenay-aux-roses, at Provins and in the marvellous gardens of Rouen, the Roman tradition had survived. In England a red rose, brought from France in the year 1200, was for centuries the symbol of the house of Lancaster, and a white rose symbolised the house of York. At the end of the 15th century, after the long and terrible Wars of the Roses, the two roses were united in the house of Tudor – and today the rose is still one of the symbols of the British royal house.

In Germany the rose had a very special symbolism. The bleeding wounds of warrior heroes were called rosebuds, the battlefield was known as a rose garden. Yet in the age of chivalry it was also connected with love, and love philters were distilled from roses.

After the medieval age Europe came to a scientific period: printing was invented in Germany and botanists studied plants as they were, not as Aristotle had described them. Roses, grown according to the principles of Albert the Great and Pietro de' Crescenzi, were used in particular as hedges, and until about 1700, new flowers superseded them in many European gardens.

In 18th-century France Joséphine Beauharnais,

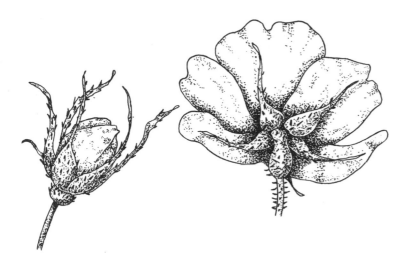

Bud with very long sepals; flower seen from below, of the *Rosa macrophylla,* showing the glandular hairs which cover the calyx.

Napoleon's wife, greatly encouraged their cultivation by creating the most famous rose garden of its time at Malmaison and commissioning the famous engraver Redouté to copy thousands of the flowers. After her death the garden was left to go wild, but the roses she had made famous continued to fascinate people and many rose gardens were planted by kings and emperors during the 19th century.

Feasts in honour of the rose were held and its cultivation was popular everywhere; the climbing varieties on walls, artificial ruins and Gothic gateways were particular favourites. People gave presents of vases shaped as pyramids or spheres, holding very neat and regular blooms all round them.

New varieties were already sold for fabulous sums during the last century, and the enthusiasm for roses has continued until our own day, when it has given rise to a specialised industry.

Today, magazines on roses, and societies of rose lovers like the National Rose Society in England, teach people how to grow the flower and maintain its popularity. Cut roses are arranged in all kinds of ways: in bunches, in baskets, or with other flowers; from America the fashion has spread for displaying a single rose in a crystal vase. Roses are suitable for every occasion and today, as in the past, they are the very best flower for every kind of decoration.

A bouquet of long-stemmed roses always makes the most charming welcome for a distinguished visitor, and it is said that the then Aga Khan sent thirty thousand roses to Geneva when the League of Nations was launched. Even in the twentieth century heads of state may be welcomed by a shower of rose petals during an official visit.

Today the rose is as much of a symbol as ever, for its harmonious beauty still represents mystery, purity and love. So many associations have made this emblem of secrecy their own, like the anti-Nazi 'White Rose' group in recent years. Its regular appearance means that it is often used emblematically, for subjects that have nothing to do with botany.

And today, as in ancient times, a bunch of red roses means a declaration of love.

We now have splendid flower shops, where we can find roses in the most varied colours and with the most superb scents. But in spring and summer we can also still enjoy the beautiful wild roses in the hedgerows and woods.

The principal wild roses

In hedges and woods, in stony places, on hills and plains in many countries, we find the delightful wild rose; sometimes this belongs to a species that has not been cultivated and has remained in its natural state. These are shrubs of the rose family and their stalks have strong curved thorns near their base.

Their leaves, which are a fine shiny green on the top side and paler on the underside, may be deciduous or evergreen, and are formed of between five and seven tiny leaves set on the axis of the leaf like the barbs of a feather. The flowers come out in May or June, singly or in pairs, on a single stem.

There are five green sepals surrounding five petals that are generally pink and occasionally white. Inside are a great many stamens, and the ovaries are in the swelling at the base of the flower.

The spurious fruit of the rose, called the hip, is generally red and in the shape of a fleshy bag, twisted at the top by the remains of the sepals and full of pips – the real fruit.

The most widespread of the wild roses is the dog-rose. It grows in hedges and woods to a height of 3000 feet above sea level, and flowers from May to July in most European countries. Its petals are pink or whitish.

In the hedges and woods of Central Europe the *Rosa arvensis* is found; it has slender reddish-mauve branches, with white flowers that bloom in June and July.

Similar to the dog-rose is the *Rosa gallica,* which forms low bushes and has beautiful scented flowers, generally deep pink but sometimes bright or deep red.

On mountain slopes, around woods, grows the *Rosa cinnamomea,* a tall bush with large pink flowers that grow singly or in groups of twos and threes. The *Rosa pendulina*

7

Buds and flower of the *Rosa involucrata:* note the completely bare stalk and calyx.

(synonymous with the *Rosa alpina)* grows higher up, and flowers from June to August; it has purplish or pink flowers and no thorns.

The flowers of the *Rosa moschata* and the *Rosa rubiginosa* have a very individual scent. The *Rosa moschata,* which has grown up naturally on the Mediterranean shores in particular, has white flowers in clusters and a musky scent; and the *Rosa rubiginosa,* which grows in stony, untended places, has resinous glands that give out a smell like russet apples.

In Italy, the *Rosa sempervirens,* which originated in the east, has become naturalised; it has white flowers, a strong scent, and blooms from May to July.

The moss rose *(Rosa centifolia muscosa),* is very beautiful and pure, and can easily be recognised because its stalks are covered with a great many small, soft prickles.

Many other species are found in Europe, Asia and America. However modest they may seem, they are all important in the cultivation of roses, because they can be crossed with already hybrid roses and many of them are used in the propagating of the cultivated species.

The cultivated roses

Through selection and hybridization, a great many types of roses have been created from the wild species. These vary in form, in colour, in the richness of their petals and in their behaviour. The roses that came to us from the east were probably the result of a great deal of selection already, and so different from their ancestors, the wild species.

Most experts believe that three species, the *Rosa centifolia muscosa,* the *Rosa gallica* and the *Rosa damascena,* came to us from south-east Asia, perhaps descended from a single common ancestor. The *centifolia* reached North Africa, Spain and the south of France and acclimatised itself perfectly, becoming the 'rose de Provence' or 'rose chou' or 'cent feuilles' of the French, and the *Rosa provincialis* of the Romans.

The ancient authors mention this rose, which later crossed the Bosphorus, passed into Germany and Holland, and was improved and widely grown.

In the next age the *Rosa gallica* came to Europe, possibly brought in by the Romans. It spread to northern France, especially to Provins, where in fact it was named the 'rose of Provins'. Its late-blooming flower had twelve generally red petals, it was cultivated all through the Middle Ages as a medicinal plant and was taken to England by the Duke of Lancaster, where it became part of the arms of the kings of England. The early settlers probably took it to America.

Another ancient rose is the rose of Damascus *(Rosa damascena),* which has individual, drooping flowers with a charming perfume. It was brought by the Greeks to Marseilles, Carthage and Paestum, and became the Romans' rose. It was in fact in Italy, at Paestum, that it was seen to be 'reflowering', that is that it bloomed twice a year, and so the Romans called it *Rosa bifera* and the French the 'rose des quatre saisons'. It was destroyed by the eruption of Vesuvius and although the Arabs cultivated it and obtained rose-water from it, it reappeared in the west only about the year 1500.

The real revolution in rose growing took place at the end of the 18th century when the roses of Bengal and China reached Europe, in particular *Rosa indica* and the *Rosa sempervirens.* These and others were discovered in Canton by merchants of the East India Company, and reached England through Holland.

The *Rosa indica,* which already had many forms, had a scent like that of tea, and so the name tea-rose was given to its large, perfectly formed flowers, with their ten, or even fifteen, petals. Its leaves, which were longlasting and resistant to disease, were a dark shiny green. The *Rosa sempervirens* or Bengal rose, which bloomed for a very long period, had white flowers that grew in clusters.

When these and other species reached Europe, and the sexuality of plants was discovered (that is, about the end of the 18th century) rose-growers were able to do what they had only dreamed about before, and the richness of forms and colours we now know was achieved through hybridisation.

Today, then, the old roses in our gardens have been

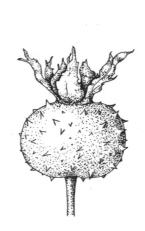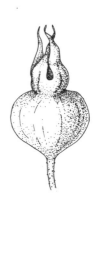

Left: Rose hip, shaped like an ampoule. Right: Spurious fruit: hip of the dog rose.

Left: Rose hip, globular, flattened top and bottom, with thorns. Right: Rose hip, globular and spiral.

joined by 'young' or 'modern' roses, less than a century old. The old roses include the original species gradually brought into Europe, and their hybrids; these are still known by their Latin names. The modern roses have been obtained by crossing the old ones and their hybrids, and are known by a special symbolism or by invented names; it is often impossible to trace their ancestors.

These new roses began to be grown in gardens in the 19th century as a result of the crossings made among the species that were already known. Then came the *Rosa bourboniana*, with its large, dark pink flowers, from the island of Réunion, and the *Rosa alba,* with its dazzlingly white petals and pleasant scent, from northern Europe. The many hybrids of all these species were called 'perpetuals', although in fact few roses really flower perpetually.

They were highly resistant to disease and achieved a wide range of colours, yet few of them have come down to us, because they were crossed with tea-roses, and formed new hybrids known as hybrid-teas which, though less healthy than their parent roses, had many-petaled, delightfully shaped flowers and were very decorative. They became very popular in gardens, where they were especially suitable for making flowerbeds.

The end of the 19th century was important in the history of the rose, for in May, 1885, a French gardener named Pernet-Ducher happened to see, in the garden of the Tête d'Or at Lyons, a branch on a rose bush with flowers that were copper and yellow. This was a mutation, or what growers call a 'sport'; where, through some trick of nature, one branch on the bush 'sports' a different colour.

These roses were a revelation to Monsieur Pernet-Ducher: in the gardens of his time there were no yellow or orange or two-toned roses.

From then onwards he spent his life seeking a yellow rose, and about forty years later, in 1920, he produced his masterpiece, 'Souvenir de Claudius Pernet', the yellow rose named after his son, who had been killed in the war.

This perfectly-formed rose, with its double flowers in a warm yellow, was the ancestor of all the reddish-orange roses and all the two-coloured roses so fashionable today.

The yellow varieties, though, perhaps because this ancestor of theirs was a delicate, greenhouse specimen, had little resistance and were short-lived. Most of them have disappeared from the catalogues but, through the use of stock with a stronger constitution, the modern yellow roses are hardy and reliable.

The climbing roses, derived through crossings from *Rosa indica* and *Rosa moschata,* began to develop at the beginning of this century. Roses of this type in our gardens today are found on bushes that cling to supports and mostly bloom only once in summer. They form good fences for protection against animals and are used, in America in particular, as anti-dazzle and crash barriers on the highways, with good effect.

Their flowers may be large, with a great many petals, or simple, with only five petals, or half-double, with a double row of petals; but they all have the one characteristic, that they grow in clusters. Some varieties, among them Dortmund, Danse de Feu, and Aloha, are suitable for small gardens, while the splendid Mermaid seems more at home in a larger garden.

By being successfully crossed with tea roses, these climbing roses have produced some dwarf roses known as Polyantha Pompoms. They were the first miniature roses, and were also called fairy roses or Lilliputians; all of them are very small, with a large number of tiny flowers in clusters, and an extremely elegant air. They have no scent, but can be grown in pots very successfully.

Later these first dwarf roses were crossed with hybrid tea roses by the Danish grower Svend Poulsen, and produced the large, strong, Poulsen roses, that is, the Polyantha hybrid roses more recently known as Floribundas.

Today, these are very popular in gardens. Their flowers grow in clusters, are formed of five or ten fleshy petals, and are remarkably resistant to disease. Quite apart from their beauty, they are popular because they are easy to grow.

They are used a great deal to form flowerbeds in which what matters most is the general effect of the colour, and they are particularly well liked by people who want the best results with the least amount of work. In recent years,

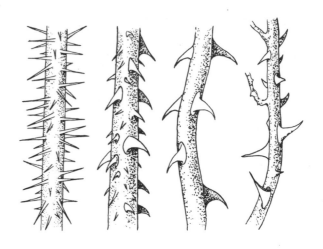

Various types of thorn on rose stems and branches: from left to right: needle-shaped thorns, beak-shaped thorns, crescent-shaped thorns pointing downwards, and beak-shaped thorns, some of which point upwards.

though, they have been crossed again with hybrid tea roses, and their forms have become much richer. Tea roses have also been improved: they are delicate but much prized, and are always shown in the most important international competitions.

The largest and the smallest rose

Whenever we look at nature we like to know which is the largest and which the smallest of each species, and it is always hard to say, when creation has so many forms. With roses, if we consider the fifteen thousand varieties that exist today, it is nearly impossible.

If by 'largest' we mean the number of petals in a rose, then certainly the Baccara rose wins: it has a maximum of seventy-two petals in flowers that are two to three inches in diameter. But the flower may have few petals, ten to fifteen, for instance, yet have a record diameter of four inches, like the red Anna Wheatcroft or the coral-pink Ascot.

Some roses, the red, scented Tally Ho, for example, or the yellow Burnaby, have flowers with a diameter of about four inches and a large number of petals as well. An effect of size is also achieved by a rose like the Ama, which has large double flowers in compact clusters and fine orange leaves.

Similarly, it is hard to choose the smallest rose: among miniature roses, the Baby Masquerade, with flowers only one inch in diameter, must be considered the smallest, and among non-dwarf roses, the smallest are roses like the Cocktail or Border Coral, which have flowers less than two inches in diameter.

The rose-bush in the garden

From early summer to late autumn the rose bush is the finest ornament of any garden, particularly suited to forming straight-sided or circular flowerbeds with roses of the floribunda type, that is, with medium-sized bushes bearing flowers in clusters that bloom regularly and constantly.

They should be planted about twelve to fifteen inches apart. Rose bushes of a single colour should be grown in each bed, with a few small rose trees to break the monotony.

These rose trees are very useful as hedges or protective borders, and so are tall rose bushes, but the distance between them must be at least a yard if they are used in this way.

Climbing roses, many of them blooming a second time, are particularly suitable for covering sunny walls and for growing round windows and doors. They must be planted from two to three and a half yards apart and given wire supports to climb over.

If pillars are to be covered, or trellises of roses formed, rambler roses are needed with small flowers that do not bloom twice but have a rich growth. A bed of roses for cut flowers is also useful in the garden, and for this hybrid tea roses with long stalks are the most suitable.

Rose-growing in pots needs expert advice; miniature roses, hybrid tea or floribundas, which can be grown in a small amount of soil, are all suitable.

Famous rose gardens and new varieties

Roses are shown to best advantage in a rose garden, that is, a sunny garden where nothing else is grown. The beds have regular geometrical shapes and are at least a yard apart; lawns show up the colour of the flowers and small rose trees, pergolas, pilasters and climbing roses provide variety and interest.

In specialised gardens, cultivators experiment, crossing species and seeking continuously, with infinite patience, for new colours such as black and delphinium blue; here they prepare the new varieties which are shown at competitions, held in the world's most famous rose centres.

Rose growers are faced with great difficulties. Each cross

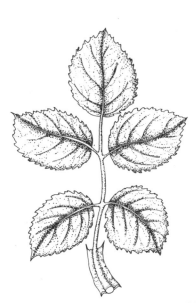

Schematic drawing of a spray of rose leaves, consisting of five small oval serrated leaves; the stalk has no thorns.

Leaf of *Rosa indica*, var. *ruga:* a hybrid between *Rosa chinensis* and *Rosa arvensis*. The stalk is prickly; as in other roses, there may be an even number of leaves because one of those in the end pair is missing.

between two roses produces an enormous number of seeds, and the same crossing often has to be repeated thousands of times. At the Meilland gardens in Antibes, for instance, forty-five thousand seeds are grown each year, and through selection, within five or six years, they must be reduced to three or four types which represent the new varieties.

Every year about two hundred new roses are produced all over the world. They must conform to certain standards of behaviour and size, and must be tried out for at least three years at the rose centre where the competition is held. The winner generally receives a large prize and is hailed as an inventor; and his variety is protected and patented.

One of the most famous rose gardens is that of the Jackson and Perkins Company at Newark (New York), which cultivates all the varieties that are sold today. In Europe there is a famous rose garden in Geneva, and the Bagatelle park in Paris, where the 'rose of the year' is chosen is well known too. In France there is also the rose garden at Lyons, where modern roses were born, and where a competition limited to French varieties is held, and the rose garden of Haÿ-les-roses, which includes a rose museum.

The most beautiful rose garden in the world is said to be that of the Oeste Park in Madrid, started from scratch in 1954. In England, there is Queen Mary's famous rose garden at Regents Park in London, and Winston Churchill's rose garden, the Golden Walk at Chartwell, planted in 1958 to celebrate his golden wedding.

In Italy, a competition is held in the rose garden in Rome, planted in 1928 on the ruins of the Domus Aurea and enlarged in 1948. Another famous rose garden is in Turin; this is part of the Valentino gardens, and was planted in 1961 to celebrate the centenary of the unification of the Kingdom of Italy.

How to grow roses

As a rule the rose has an important quality – through its wide distribution it is adaptable and that is why it can be found in most gardens. It prefers a heavy loam and will thrive remarkably well in very clayey soil.

Preparation of the ground must be thorough, and for rose beds a trench, approximately 18 inches wide, should be taken out one end and the soil deposited at the other end of the bed, ready for filling in. Make certain the bottom of the trench is well broken up, incorporating some organic manure in doing so, and then turn in the next 18 inches of soil, mixing with it a liberal application of well-rotted manure. This should be done as early in the autumn as possible, for the ground to settle before planting, leaving it in a rough condition.

Planting may begin immediately after leaf fall, which may be from mid-November. The site should be dressed with 'hoof and horn' or basic slag at ¾ ounces per square yard and then broken up to a fine tilth. If roses arrive from the nurseryman with their roots in a dry condition, they should be thoroughly soaked before planting. Dig a hole sufficiently wide to spread the roots and firm well. If planted correctly, the budded part – which is easily discernible – should be at soil level.

Established beds should be dressed with bonemeal in February, gently hoeing it in. From the end of April until mid-July dress with a proprietary rose mixture at fortnightly intervals, following the maker's instructions strictly. At each application lightly hoe the fertiliser in.

Rose beds should be hoed frequently throughout the season, to control weeds and conserve moisture, or, if desired, mulched, sphagnum peat being the tidiest method. This also suppresses weeds and retains moisture and, what is important, helps to maintain an even soil temperature.

Pests and diseases

There are not many pests that can cause damage to the rose. An infestation of aphids may descend on the young growths at an early stage and at the same time, or a little later, caterpillars may be detected on the leaves. Usually, with the latter, they are few and may be picked off and destroyed. Pesticides are available to control both.

Sudden changes in temperature will bring an attack of mildew at any time. Once noticed, this can be controlled by

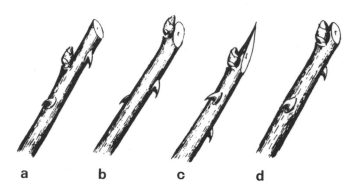

Some of the wrong ways (a, b, c) and the right way (d) of pruning. Facing page (top): a rose bush before pruning, with tangled branches and weak growth; the same bush thinned out; and a hybrid tea pruned to within 6 inches of the ground, with the buds left pointing outwards to make a shapely bush. The diagrams (facing, below) show how grafting is carried out. **1:** The bud is just visible in the axil of the leaf. **2–3:** A sliver of bark is removed with the bud and the axil. **4–5:** The wood from the inside of the bark is removed, and the piece trimmed neatly at each end. **6–8:** A neat T cut is made in the bark of the stock, the bud is slipped in, and tied tightly in place with raffia so that all air is excluded. New growth soon follows.

spraying with sulphur compound. Continue this throughout the season at fortnightly intervals.

More serious are the fungus diseases, which, if ignored, may result in partial or complete loss of foliage. These are rust and black spots both of which do not appear much before August. However, the rose lover may prevent this by using a proprietary fungicide spray every ten days from the beginning of May. It is best to consult a reliable supplier for his advice as to the most suitable fungicide, and use according to instructions.

Pruning of roses

Pruning is necessary to encourage healthy growth, which, in turn, promotes good blooms. It also maintains a shapely bush but it must be expertly done. Arguments have raged and will continue to do so, as to the best time to commence. Generally speaking, the end of February is a good starting point, according to the season – all pruning must be suspended during frosty weather – and bearing in mind that the further north one goes, so it becomes progressively later.

Hybrid Teas   A start should be made with the hybrid teas; first remove all weak growth and shorten the remainder from three to five buds, according to strength, always cutting to an outward facing eye. Vigorous varieties should be more lightly pruned. Newly planted bushes should be cut to soil level, to encourage root action and robust growth.

Floribundas   Here, the young growths should have a few inches removed from the tip. The older wood may be removed altogether, according to the number of young growths, or if left, shortened to two or three buds. New bushes should have all growths reduced to about 6 inches.

Ramblers   Prune in late summer after flowering. If there is sufficient new growth – five to seven – remove all old wood. Where the previous year's growth has to be retained, spur hard back to one or two buds. Newly planted ramblers should be cut back to one foot.

Climbers   Remove all weak growth. Retain the young growth and older wood where necessary. Do not prune or cut back for one year after planting.

Standards   Prune as for hybrid teas and floribundas. Keep a sharp watch for growth from stem of the stock and remove immediately.

Weeping Standards   These are rambler roses budded at the top of five to six foot stems, the strong growths reaching to the ground. Most effective where umbrella wire trainers are used. Prune as for ramblers, tipping the young growth.

Rose species   No pruning required, except to remove dead or very weak wood.

Old-fashioned roses   After the first year, cut out dead or weak wood and crossed branches. It may be essential at times to remove some branches altogether, to give the tree air and light.

Summer pruning   When dead-heading roses, it is more advantageous to remove one-third of the growth at the same time. This encourages stronger growth from the base of the bush.

Autumn pruning   This is not really pruning at all, but the reduction of all strong growth by approximately half to prevent wind-rocking. This is a cause of many fatalities amongst roses during the winter months.

Removal of suckers   Suckers are those growths coming from the stock below where the bud was inserted, distinguishable by their different appearance or number of leaflets – seven. It is customary to cut these off at ground level, but this only encourages more growth, to the detriment of the host. The soil should be carefully moved and the shoot traced to its base. Hold firmly, tug sharply and it should become detached from the root. Replace soil immediately and firm well.

12

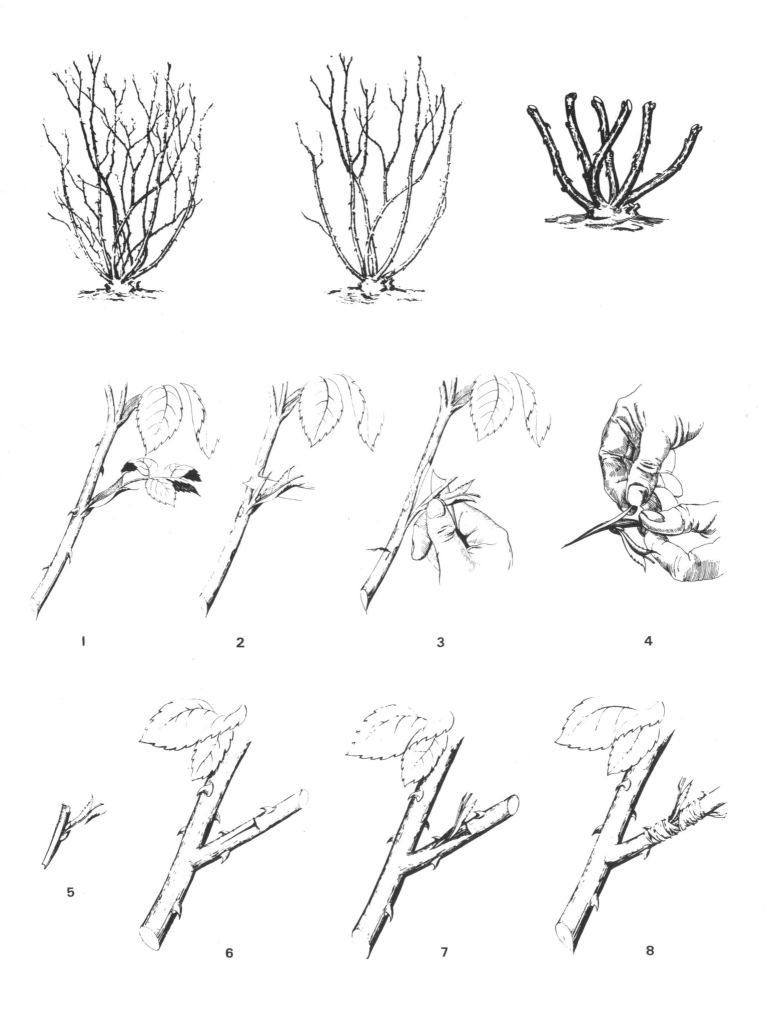

1   2   3   4

5   6   7   8

The rose in human life

In ancient times and in the Middle Ages love philters were made from roses; but quite apart from this magical use, roses were used as excellent deodorants, in times when washing was unfashionable. Even today, small sachets of dried rose petals are sometimes still put in the linen cupboard.

In ancient Rome, roses were used in the preparation of jellies, honey, wine and desserts, and today the fruit of the dog rose is used to make preserves and jam. In the east, their petals are used in the making of sweets and to flavour liqueurs and ice-creams.

The important medicinal qualities of roses were already known in Roman times, and in the Middle Ages all apothecaries used them because their fruit was rich in what we now know as vitamin C.

Today rose water has a pharmaceutical use in the cure of eye diseases; the petals of the *Rosa centifolia* are used in laxatives for children, and those of the *Rosa gallica* provide astringent liquids and are used in rose hip syrup.

Rose water and essences made from roses are most useful of all in the perfume industry, which came to us from the east – from Arabia and Persia in particular. Rose water is extracted from the *Rosa moschata* and the *Rosa damascena,* by rapid distillation with steam or a solvent, and this is used to purify and improve the skin; distilled again, it becomes an essence used in perfumes.

The perfume industry is important in Nice and Cannes, and even more so in Eastern Europe and the near east – in Bulgaria and Turkey mainly; but recently the production of artificial essences has hit it hard.

The rose in this century is important as a decoration, and thousands of people, including rose experts, are employed in producing cut flowers, potted bushes and garden plants. The Dutch, who produce flowers that are entirely uniform and very predictable in their behaviour and quality, are supremely successful in the cultivation of roses. Their rivals are the South Africans.

The rose in art

In a few lines it is impossible to deal adequately with the broad subject of the rose in art. Every form of art, poetry, painting, sculpture, interior decoration, has been influenced by the rose and continues to be so.

Since ancient times poets have praised the rose and used it as a symbol of youth, of the beloved, of the fleetingness of earthly things and of vanity. This began with Sappho, continued through Virgil, the *Roman de la Rose,* Poliziano and Lorenzo the Magnificent, and still survives today.

Other artists have found the rose a subject worthy of contemplation and love. It is engraved on ancient coins and painted in the frescoes of Pompeii; we find it in Flemish and Renaissance paintings, on Gothic gates or musical instruments.

The best way of ending a book on roses is to mention once again the French engraver Redouté, whose copies of the roses in the Empress Josephine's garden at Malmaison are unsurpassed.

Principal roses, listed by colour

White roses
Frau Karl Druschki: A vigorous bush with white flowers, sometimes pink in the centre.
Iceberg: A vigorous bush with flat double flowers in scented clusters.

Yellow roses
Buccaneer: A useful bush for borders, with scented flowers.
Allgold: A bush with flowers that grow singly or in groups.

Apricot-coloured roses
Bayadère: A vigorous bush with large double flowers.

Pale pink roses
Grace of Monaco: A bush of large, round, scented flowers.
Pearl of Montserrat: A miniature rose bush.

Salmon-coloured roses
Border Coral: A vigorous bush with flowers in scented sprays.

Deep pink roses
Aloha: A small reflowering tree with scented flowers.

Red roses
Danse des Sylphes: A climbing and reflowering bush.

Roses with scarlet touches
Baccara: The commonest red rose.

Dark red roses
Pigalle: A vigorous bush with large, full flowers.

Two-coloured roses
Masquerade: A vigorous bush with flowers that may fade from yellow to pink and dark red.

Lavender-coloured roses
Lilac Time: A bush with full, lilac flowers.

1

2

3

1 *Rosa pendulina (= Rosa alpina)* is found mostly, but not always, in mountainous country, and its flowers, which have touches of purple about them, bloom between June and August.

2 The flowers have faded and the leaves have fallen, but the wild rose's thorny stalk is now decorated with its spurious red fruit, the hips. Their curious bag-shaped form makes them useful in unconventional flower arrangements, and their high vitamin C content makes them very nutritious; they are still used to make preserves and jam.

3 One of the flowers that tells us that summer has come in June is the dog rose, which grows in woods, on high land or at sea-level. Delicate and elegant on their spiny stalks, the five pink petals surround the small stamens and central pistil, and green leaves form their background, sometimes shining and sometimes pale.

4–5 In 1590 the *Rosa moschata* reached the shores of the Mediterranean from far-away Persia. Its strong, straight stalks have stout reddish thorns, and its white flowers, often tinged with pink, have a mossy scent, much used in the making of perfumes.
The buds shown in the two illustrations are moss roses *(Rosa centifolia muscosa)*, not to be confused with the one just described. Their stalks and sepals are entirely covered in small soft prickles; and they are deep pink, often lightly streaked with bright red.

6 This rose *(Rosa spinosissima altaica)* is a fine example of the queen of flowers: its pale petals form an elegant cup with a golden base. Stamens and pistils form a delicate halo in various shades of gold and even when the flower has been turned into fruit this is still preserved for a very long time.

7 White Queen is a suitable name for this glorious, glowing bud, a hybrid tea with delicate white flowers. The central part of the flower is rather long, and its upstanding carriage makes it seem really queenly.

8 Dagmar Spath is one of the most decorative floribundas. The flowers, which have a large number of petals, are open against the dark, shiny green leaves, their many delicate stamens giving them a golden heart.

9 A cool whiteness characterises this very beautiful floribunda, suitably named Iceberg. The flowers, which grow in abundant clusters, have a large number of petals that cling closely together for a long time before opening into a splendid cup. This is a vigorous, healthy flower, which grows on a bush that has many branches and plenty of light green leaves.

8

9

11

10

10 This slightly scented rose, the Queen Elizabeth, was created in 1955. It has large double flowers with very centralised petals; the buds are carmine, but when they open into flowers their colour becomes lighter and softer, contrasting with the dark shiny green of the leathery leaves. The bush is straight and vigorous, and particularly suited to forming hedges.

11 Various shades of pink and red are found in the petals of this elegant hybrid tea named Percy Thrower. The leaves are gleaming and the petals tend to curl outwards.

12 Nothing can honour the great Dr. Schweitzer better than this hybrid tea named after him. The perfect open flower is dark pink, shading into lighter, more delicate colours on the edges.

13

13 It's very light pink, slightly darker at the centre, and its disdainful way of holding itself, make the name Royal Highness very suitable for this rose. The scented flowers stand up very straight, the petals cling tightly round the bud, and the dark, gleaming, leathery leaves make a halo around them.

14 This hybrid tea, Princess Margaret, has full, perfectly formed flowers and a large number of petals. It is a brilliant pink, which is particularly splendid on the papery exterior of the petals.

15 Invitation is the name of this elegant hybrid tea. The flowers are double and the tightly packed petals are deep pink, faintly tinged with yellow near the base. There are many stiff, bright green leaves.

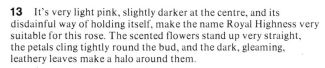

14

15

16 Mischief is the name of this beautiful, and quite unmischievous, hybrid tea. Its flowers are perfectly formed and as much as 4 inches in diameter when they are completely open. The basic colour is pink, but with an orange tinge at the edges.

17 Jenny Fair, a hybrid tea, has very beautiful pale pink petals, curling slightly outwards to form a large, perfect flower.

18 City of Leeds is the name of this floribunda. The flowers hold
themselves up straight and the scented petals are an intense,
classic pink.

19 This floribunda, named Love Token, has large double flowers. In the mature flower the petals are wide open, showing the golden stamens. The leaves look leathery, and are a warm coppery colour.

20 Super Star really is the star of the roses in its group – the hybrid teas. Its slightly scented flowers with their many petals, carried on a long stalk with fine dark shining leaves, its lovely shape and medium size, all make it one of the varieties that rose lovers most delight in.

19

20

21 Tip-Top is the light-hearted name of this deep pink floribunda. Its flowers are large and compact, and when its many petals open up they have a cup-shaped form.

22 Dearest is the name of this floribunda, with cup-shaped flowers that often have as many as thirty petals. Their light pink colour contrasts with the dark green of the leaves and their very sweet scent makes them particularly prized.

23 Elizabeth of Glamis is a well known variety of floribunda. The flowers always stand up straight and the dominating colour, a deep pink, fades slightly on the edges of the petals, which curl outwards when the flower is completely open. The leaves are a delicate green.

25

2

24 Vilia is a classic floribunda with simple, medium-sized flowers in small, charming clusters. The petals are pale scarlet, veined at the base with light yellow, and the flowers have a delicate scent.

25 Tombola is a gay name for this variety of floribunda, the result of many patient crossings. The flowers, which have a lot of petals, are bright pink, faintly tinged with yellow, and are compactly shaped for a long time before they open out into a large cup.

26 My Girl is an affectionate name for a delightful floribunda. It has large flowers, with many intensely pink petals, and fine, bright green leaves.

27 The flowers of the floribunda Pink Parfait are medium sized, but they are double and quite perfect. The basic colour, pale pink, seems to deepen at the edges and shade into crimson. The back of the petals, on the other hand, is a pale, very delicate apricot colour. The flowers have a faint scent and are surrounded by abundant light green leaves. The way the buds hold themselves is also charming.

26

27

28 Fragrant Cloud is the name of this hybrid tea. The double flowers are perfectly shaped and consist of fleshy, velvety petals in an exquisite tone of deep pink.

29 The hybrid tea Papa Gontier has a form that is all its own. It is double, and a delicate pink, but what is characteristic of it is the way its petals curl round on themselves lengthways, giving the whole an untidy appearance. The leaves are a fine shiny green, while the buds and stalks are reddish.

30 The variety Madame Heny has flowers of a delicate pink carried on long stalks. With the lovely structure of its double flower, and its close-knit petals, it is probably one of the best roses for use as cut flowers.

31 The variety called Simon holds itself straight and has clusters of three or four flowers at the end of its stalks. These flowers are double, with closely set petals and an amazing colour. The basic colour is a very pale pink, shading on the edges to a pale, delicate lilac that pervades the whole flower, giving it a remarkable appearance. The intensely green, gleaming leaves make it all the more striking.

32 Blue Moon is the poetic name a grower gave a hybrid tea variety of a really extraordinary, almost moonlit shade. The flower is large, double and finely shaped; the petals, which in the bud are slightly pink, have a different tone, a kind of pale yellow, when they open. The result is unexpected and attractive, and dark shining leaves form its background.

29 30

32

33 Chrysler Imperial is the name of this hybrid tea, with large full flowers and a magnificent form; they may have as many as forty to fifty petals of an intense, glowing crimson. The buds are long and tight and the leaves abundant and intensely green. This rose was created in 1952, and is very compact and robust.

34 One of the loveliest hybrid teas is romantically called First Love. Its flowers have about twenty-five scented petals which first form a delicate long bud and then open into a pale pink flower, shading into darker tones. The bush is vigorous, upstanding, bears many flowers and has light green leaves. The blooms are popular as cut flowers, because they stand up straight and are delicately formed.

33

34

35

36

35 The large flowers of Manitou have warm, velvety red petals which contrast with the golden yellow of the anthers and the shining green of the leaves. Its many petals spread and fold outwards, making the flower seem broad and open.

36 A cultivated dog rose. It has kept the appearance of a wild rose, and its flowers are simple, but their colour is intense and they hold themselves straight, in clusters, thus showing the patient care of some cultivator.

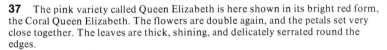

38

37   The pink variety called Queen Elizabeth is here shown in its bright red form, the Coral Queen Elizabeth. The flowers are double again, and the petals set very close together. The leaves are thick, shining, and delicately serrated round the edges.

38   Paprika is a suitable name for this vivid, geranium-red floribunda. The flowers are semi-double and often have a beautiful bluish streak at the base of their petals. It is a vigorous, strong variety bearing plenty of flowers and thick, shiny, very decorative dark leaves.

39   A floribunda with double flowers, charmingly named Maria. The flowers grow in clusters on their stalks and the petals are folded untidily against the dark green background of the leaves.

40   Evelyn Fison is a floribunda with a bushy, compact appearance. The flowers grow in clusters, set slightly apart from one another; they are large, and surrounded by small, light green leaves, faintly scented, with a great many petals, and a brilliant scarlet. When they are open they may be as much as three inches in diameter.

39   **40**

41

41 Wendy Cussons appeared in 1959 and is a vigorous bush with many branches and shiny dark green leaves. The flower is long like that of other hybrid teas, and can have as many as thirty-seven closely set petals. It has a great many flowers which are prized for their strong scent and velvety cherry-red colour.

42

43

42 This hybrid tea is known as Coralita, and its dominating colour is actually coral. The flowers are double and have closely set petals, and the small leaves are leathery, dark and shiny.

43 This very beautiful rose is a glowing velvety red, and, perhaps in memory of the rose of Lancaster, it is called Lancastrian. The flower is double, with scented petals, at the base of which is a touch of yellow; the leaves are intensely green.

44 Broad, bright red flowers with many petals grow in clusters on stalks that seem to be bending under their weight. The leaves grow thickly and are a delicate, attractive green.

45 A decisive, velvety red is the colour of this floribunda, Strawberry Fair. The flowers are double, and the closely set petals open out into a large cup when the flower is mature, worthily framed by dark green leaves.

44

45

46

47

46 This hybrid tea, created by Meilland in 1959, was named after the famous French dress-designer Christian Dior. The rose carries itself well and its flowers are perfectly formed and slightly scented; their crimson colour stands out against a background of abundant, intensely green leaves.

47 And here is the most famous red rose of all – Baccara. Its flowers have as many as seventy-two petals, which curve prettily outwards when they open. Its characteristic colour is an intense, brilliant geranium-red, and its leaves are tough and dark green. The bush bears a great many flowers and is commercially grown under glass. Its blooms are particularly popular as cut flowers, and last a very long time.

48 Finale is a floribunda with bright red flowers, which grow in thick clusters on the ends of their stalks and have a large number of petals. This is a handsome plant with plenty of shiny green leaves.

49 Lili Marlene is the name of this fine floribunda, created in 1959 It has large semi-double flowers with as many as twenty bright carmine petals; they grow in thick clusters and have a faint scent. The bush is vigorous, with many branches and plenty of leaves.

50

50 This hybrid tea is called Champs Elysées after the most famous street in Paris, where the great parades and ceremonies are held. It was produced in 1957, is vigorous, upstanding and produces plenty of large, double, deep crimson flowers, slightly scented and with a cup-shaped form.

51 Uncle Walter is the name given by its creator, McGredy, to this hybrid tea in 1963. The bush is robust and gives good results even when grown in a pot; and the fiery red flowers, borne on stout stems and slow to fade, have a perfect form.

51

52

53

52 Orange Sensation has medium sized flowers but they are double and full. It is a floribunda created in 1960, with a vigorous, bushy appearance, and plenty of fine, dark green leaves. The flowers are delicately scented, orange in colour, sometimes with vermilion streaks on the edge of the petals.

53 The floribunda called Orangeade, produced in 1959, has full, semi-double flowers which flatten as they open out. The buds are vermilion but turn to orange in the open flower and then, when it is about to fade, turn reddish again. The scent is weak, but the plant is strong and has plenty of branches.

54 Orange is the dominant colour in the flowers of the variety Spanish Orange, although there are pink or red touches on the buds and at the base of the petals. The flowers have a large number of petals which widen and flatten against the dark green background of the leaves when they open out.

55 Ramon Back has some lovely elusive tones among the orangey-yellow at the base of the petals and the pale pink at their edges. The flowers are double, medium sized and well shaped, the leaves small and closely packed, and an attractive deep green.

56 The flower of the variety Beauté, created in 1953, is so perfect that it really seems to represent beauty itself. The colour is attractive and unexpected: an orange that shades from light to dark. The flowers are double and scented, but the plant, which belongs to the hybrid tea group, is not really vigorous or resistant.

57 Apricot is the name of this tea rose, because of its unusual colour. The long flowers have very tightly packed petals with all kinds of other tones in them: delicate red streaks on the edges, for instance. The leaves are a dark shiny green, sometimes bordering on a coppery colour.

56

57

58

58 This variety of floribunda with an open, flattened flower has a superb colour, somewhere between pale pink and a number of orange tones. The stalk is long and bears dark green leaves.

59 Cover Girl is the name of this magnificent rose. The flower is double and compact, and its petals are superbly subtle in colour. The light yellow of the base is crossed by slender vermilion lines, thicker on the outside of the petals than elsewhere and fading when the flower is completely open. The leaves are a tender green.

59

60

61

60 A fine yellow rose, with healthy flowers and petals, slender curving branches and small, shiny green leaves.

61 Vienna Charm is the name of this tea rose. The flowers, which are double and well-shaped, have warm golden petals faintly touched with pink and open delightfully into the shape of a cup. The leaves are a dark, shiny green.

62 Amarillo is the name of a beautiful hybrid tea variety with double closely packed flowers. They are a warm luminous yellow, veined with red, backed by bright green leaves.

63 This hybrid tea, Dr. A. J. Verhage, created in 1961, is a descendant of the red Baccara. Its scented, double flowers are perfectly formed and a delicate shade of yellow that contrasts with the dark green leaves. But the plant is not very vigorous.

63

64

64 One of the most famous of the yellow roses is the variety Buccaneer, which is a fine buttercup colour. The flowers are scented and although they are small they may have a great many petals in the form of a cup. The leaves are leathery, often coppery green in colour. The plant develops remarkably well and is suitable for hedges and borders.

65 The floribunda Arthur Bell has compact, closely packed flowers, with many petals and a beautiful shape. The yellow colour fades to delicate lighter tones on the edges, and the leaves are pale green on one side, and coppery on the other.

65

66 Golden Treasure is the name of this floribunda, the flowers of which are a warm, luminous shade of gold. The flowers are double and their petals, which at first are tightly packed, tend to open out untidily, surrounded by dark shiny leaves.

67 King's Ransom is the name of this really regal-looking tea rose. The flowers are closely packed and compact and an intense golden colour which fades to more delicate tones at the edges. They are faintly scented, and hold themselves straight, which shows they belong to a vigorous bush.

68 Golden Jewel is a suitable name for this exquisite variety of floribunda produced in 1959. The flowers are middle-sized, and grow in clusters. It is a small bush with many branches and dark shiny leaves.

67

68

70

 This floribunda, China Town, is a robust plant that can grow to remarkable size. Its flowers are large, with petals like those of a hybrid tea, scented and an intense yellow. The dark green leaves are large and leathery.

0 The yellow rose Norris Pratt combines the abundant flowers of floribunda, which it is, with the many petals of a hybrid tea. The flowers are a warm luminous yellow and fade very slowly. The abundant leaves are deep green and the plant is very vigorous.

71 A descendant of the yellow rose Buccaneer, this hybrid tea is named after the famous dance Bossa Nova. At first the plant seems to be a climber, then it definitely takes on the form of a bush. The flowers are yellow, with pinkish touches in the bud, and the thick leaves are a gleaming green.

72 Mary Poppins has given her name to this beautiful, gay yellow rose. The flower is large and double and the petals are tidy and closely packed. They are a pale, gleaming yellow that stands out against the dark shiny foliage.

72

7

73 The variety Baby Masquerade has flowers that are barely one inch in diameter but are double and open. Their colour is like that of the larger variety, a fine golden yellow with touches of pink and red, and they have a delicate, fruity scent. The leaves are dark green and leathery and make these roses particularly attractive; it is one of the most popular of the miniature forms.

74 Coraline is the name of this bright coral-red rose. The flowers are double, open and have many petals, set off by the intense, brilliant green of the leaves.

73

74

75

76

75 Simple Simon has bright red double flowers; the colour is deeper in the centre but the outer petals are a delicate pink. When they are completely out the flowers are wide and flat and stand out against the charming shiny little leaves.

76 June Time is the name of this miniature variety which has deep pink buds opening out into a delicate cup with a lighter tone. The dark green leaves are abundant and shiny.

77 The variety Eleanor is a small plant but its flowers have a large number of petals, set close together to give the flower an elegant, elongated form. Their colour is a glowing pink, and the large leaves are dark green.

78 The glowing red and the long, double structure of the flowers makes this plant like a small scarlet jewel. Its creator must have thought so when he christened it Miniature Scarlet Gem.

77

78

79

79   Yellow Doll is the name of this miniature variety. The outer petals curl gaily outwards, which makes them pull untidily away from the rest. The long green sepals wrap themselves round the flower as if to protect its delicate yellow tones.

80   The many petals of this variety, Baby Darling, have a touch of yellow at the base, but near the top they shade into pink, which becomes deeper and denser.

81   This not very expensive sounding rose is modestly called New Penny. It is a beautiful, delicate pink, with a great many petals that spread untidily out round the bud, showing their small yellow stamens. It is a popular flower, much sought after.

82   Little Flirt is the name of this rose with full, double flowers and petals that open wide. The buds are a glowing yellow, but when they open the yellow withdraws to the hidden parts of the flower, giving way to bright red.

80

81

82

83 Fire King is as regal and flaming as its name. The form is a perfect cup, and its rich, abundant petals make it highly prized. The leaves are shiny and a fine deep green.

84

85

84 Golden-yellow, pink, all shades of red with touches of lilac, can be seen in this bunch of miniature roses. All the flowers are small but they have a good many petals and a perfect shape.

85 Modern Times is the name of this modern flower with large, semi-double flowers whose petals tend to curl outwards. The most striking thing about it is its colour; white stripes alternating with wide bands of bright red. This rich effect was probably achieved by the technique of atomic radiation.

86

86 The outer petals in this rose are a delicate pale pink, and the inner ones deep red. The flower is large, decorated with pale green leaves.

87

88

7 The petals of the rose Bonanza are remarkable for their gorgeous colour. The deep yellow of e base turns to a delicate orange-pink higher up, and at the top is definitely red. The flower stands straight; its petals are closely packed but tend to curl outwards when it is completely open. The aves are a dark shiny green.

8 Bajazzo was created in 1962, a fine variety of hybrid tea in new colours. The petals, which are urple on the inside, are completely white on the reverse and form very large, double, compact owers. Because the petals are very closely packed, the central part keeps the pointed form of the ud. The flowers have an extremely pleasant scent and grow on a straight vigorous bush with fine iny leaves.

89 This lively looking rose is named Charleston, after the city of parties and dancing. Its petals
are yellow, edged with bright red, and wavily formed. The flower is semi-double, and, when it is
flowering, wide and flat. Its bright colour and abundant flowers, surrounded by small, shiny,
intensely green leaves, make it a really marvellous variety of floribunda.

90 Circus is the name of this floribunda, created in 1956, and it certainly suggests something bright and cheerful. The flower is medium-sized and very compact but has many petals. Its basic colour is yellow, but has scarlet speckles in the bud, and pink and delicate orange tints in the open flower. The charm of this variety lies in its scent and in the way the flowers cluster on the ends of the branches. The plant is vigorous, has a bushy appearance and is decorated with curious opaque leaves.

91 In 1951 the rose Doreen, a hybrid tea variety appeared. The flowers are double, finely shaped and an intense orange, with delicate touches of scarlet on the edges of the petals. The leaves are dark, sometimes reddish and rather large. But the bush itself is not very robust.

92 Piccadilly appeared in 1959. Its large flowers, with often as many as eighteen or twenty petals, are very compact and slightly scented. The inner side of the petal is a brilliant pink while the outside is definitely yellow. It is a vigorous upstanding bush belonging to the large group of hybrid teas, with thickly growing dark green leaves.

93 Stella is the name of this rose with large double flowers, closely packed petals and a perfect form. The background of the petals is a creamy colour which shades into pink on the edges and then grows darker and deeper until it becomes carmine. The bush is extremely vigorous and erect, and has a thick foliage of fine dark green leaves.

94 Inevitably, perhaps, there is a rose called Westminster, a hybrid tea obtained in 1959, with large, full, round, strongly scented flowers. The dominating colour is cherry red, but towards the outside the petals have lighter tones and are marked with yellow. The bush has many branches and leathery medium-sized leaves of an intense green.

95 Summer Rainbow is certainly the right name for this glorious hybrid tea with large, many-petalled flowers in delicate tones of pink and yellow. The plant stands up straight; the flower is particularly elegant in shape and blooms abundantly.

94

95

96

97

96 Another hybrid tea with petals in two colours. As a rule the buds are completely red, but when the petals move away from one another a deep yellow is visible on the outside. Its leaves make a striking background for it.

97 This hybrid tea, called Eden Rose, which appeared in 1953, has large double, strongly scented flowers. The dominant colour is deep pink which sometimes grows lighter, particularly on the back of the petals. The leaves are green, shiny and dark and the plant is an upstanding bush.

98   This tall, strong rose tree, with abundant, brightly coloured leaves, is called Mojave, after the desert in SE California. Its flowers are very large with as many as twenty-five petals, and are scented. Its dominant colours are deep orange and flame-red.

99   Firebeam is the name of this rose whose yellow petals are edged with dark red as if they had been burnt. There are a great many flowers, semi-double, with petals that tend to remain close together and give it the shape of a cup. Light shiny green leaves form its background.

98

99

100

100 The petals of the Rose Gaujard have marvellously subtle colours, ranging from creamy white to lilac pink. The lovely semi-double flowers stand up straight, surrounded by shiny leaves.

101 In this floribunda, created by Kordes in 1965, the buds are red faintly tinged with lavender, and when the flower is completely open this lavender shade is intensified, which accounts for its name, Lavendula. It flowers abundantly and the growth is erect and vigorous.

101

102 What is most striking in this variety is the large number of buds and flowers. Grouped in clusters, pressed against one another, sometimes open and sometimes completely shut, they are a slightly orange pink, which is much darker and redder in the buds.

103 In this plant the flowers grow in clusters on the ends of the branches and have a large number of petals. Their whitish-cream colour shades, sometimes at the edges, and sometimes at the base of the petals, into a warm velvety red that stands out against the shiny green of the leaves. The petals themselves open out to form a wide cup-shaped flower.

02

103

104

105

106

107

107 This hybrid tea is named after Margot Fonteyn. Its flowers are beautifully formed, deep pink with paler edges, but darker tones in the bud. When they are put in a vase of water their scent is so strong that it fills the whole room.

108 Colour Wonder is the name of this hybrid tea with a strange, original colour. The petals are salmon pink on the inside, and yellow on the outside, and are particularly well set off by olive-green leaves. This rose won the Gold Medal in Belfast as the best hybrid tea of 1966.

104 The flowers of this yellow rose grow in tight clusters surrounded by thick leaves of a very shiny bright green. The petals are a delicate yellow and stay folded for a very long time, keeping the pointed form of the bud at the centre of the flower.

105 Geisha Girl is the name of this hybrid tea. The flower is double, perfectly formed and an intense, glowing yellow. The leaves are dark green and shiny or else have a coppery tinge.

106 A beautifully formed flower that stands up straight and has petals set close together for a long way, then turning back at the top; pale yellow and darker on the reverse of the petals.

108

109

109   This very robust hybrid tea is called Wisbech Gold and has flowers in charming clusters. Every flower is large, double and has golden-yellow petals with bright red edges. The general effect is extremely original and luxurious.

110   Zambra is the name of this floribunda, which has a bushy appearance and medium-sized flowers in clusters. The petals spread and give the flower a flattened form. They are a glowing orange-pink, often shading into bright red; the green of the leaves is splendid too, and the flowers have a delicate scent.

111   This is an example of the way in which roses can be used in their many forms: red and yellow Masquerade roses form the bushy base of a flowerbed, while a vigorous, perpetual flowering yellow rose fills the space between the two windows, adding a touch of gaiety.

110

112 Black Velvet is the name of this hybrid tea whose petals are dark red, with velvety gleams. The flowers are double, and beautifully shaped, and their amazing colour contrasts with the shining green of the leaves.

113 The variety Pernille Poulsen has flowers in clusters at the ends of its branches. They are medium-sized, finely shaped, and the petals remain closely packed for a long time. The red buds grow lighter and more luminous when the flower is completely open. It has thick, plentiful, shiny green leaves.

114 The hybrid tea Brasilia is named after the new capital of Brazil. It is descended from the rose Piccadilly and keeps its main characteristics, but the colour is more intense and there is a greater contrast between the bright red of the petals and the yellow that is revealed on them when the flower opens completely. The leaves are dark green and particularly shiny.

112

113

115

116

115 Pink Perpetué is the name of a fine variety of climbing rose. The flowers, which are double and very numerous, are perfectly formed and their middle is still pointed when the outer petals have moved away from it. The buds are red, but become much lighter and more delicate when the flower is completely open. The leaves, which are not very large, are shiny and dark green, and the stalks tend to be reddish. Flowers and leaves are so abundant and long lasting that it is a very useful plant to have in a garden.

116 The variety Border Coral has medium-sized double flowers and an excellent shape. Their colour, deep pink in the central part of the flower, becomes darker on the edges – the colour of coral, as the name suggests. It flowers abundantly and the leaves are particularly attractive because they are dark green and very shiny.

117

117 These red roses, suitable for forming cascades of flowers and covering trellises, are very decorative in a garden. The flowers are large and double, with petals that tend to spread out gaily and untidily. They flower abundantly and have a large number of small, intensely green leaves, finely serrated along the edges.

118 The variety Etude may have taken a long time to produce; in any case, the result is very beautiful. The semi-double flowers open in the form of a cup surrounded by the yellow tufts of the stamens. The buds are bright green but the open flower is a delicate pink, suffused here and there with touches of red. The small, abundant leaves are dark and shiny.

118

119

121 A trellis of roses is the best screen against strong sunshine, particularly when the roses are ⟨a⟩ rich as they are in this illustration and a delicate, restful pink. These are called Parade.

122 Bantry Bay is the name of this fine climbing rose with semi-double flowers in charming clusters. The petals are a delicate pink, and the leaves abundant and dark. It is hardy and grows vigorously.

123 Sympathie is the name the rose-grower Kordes gave this climber when he created it in 1966 Its flowers have many closely-packed petals and are dark red, glowing like velvet. The plant is perpetual flowering, vigorous in growth and disease resistant.

119 Autumn Sunlight is a good name for a rose with flowers in soft warm colours. The petals are red with touches of orange, the leaves are shiny and an intense green; the buds are remarkable for their bright red colour. The flowers are double and compact, perfectly cup-shaped, and grow abundantly on the plant.

120 The flowers of the rambler Golden Showers are always completely golden. They grow thickly, are large and double and when they open they flatten into wide cup shapes, flowering one after another, either singly or in clusters. They are faintly scented, and their narcissus-yellow colour stands out against the dark gleaming background of leaves.

120

121

123

124

125

124-5 Every town likes to boast a rose garden where the beauty of roses, and the multiplicity of their forms, can be appreciated fully. When this is impossible a corner of the public park may have roses grown in it, just as happens in more modest gardens, and a path is decorated and shaded with fine climbing roses (in illustration 124, it is the variety Voie Lactée). How wonderful are their colours, their abundance, their uninterrupted flowering: nothing is pleasanter than to wander among them.